KATY
AND THE
BIG SNOW

STORY AND PICTURES
BY
VIRGINIA LEE BURTON

SCHOLASTIC INC.
New York Toronto London Auckland Sydney

Books by Virginia Lee Burton

KATY AND THE BIG SNOW

THE LITTLE HOUSE

CALICO, THE WONDER HORSE
or The Saga of Stewy Slinker

MIKE MULLIGAN AND HIS STEAM SHOVEL

CHOO CHOO

ISBN 0-590-04792-2

45 44 43 42 41   13 14 15 16 17/0

Printed in the U.S.A

To
Johnneeeeee
from Jinneeeeeeee

Katy was a beautiful red crawler tractor.
She was very big and very strong
and she could do a lot of things.

Katy had a bulldozer
to push dirt around with.

The Highway Department repaired the roads in the summer
and kept them clear of snow in the winter
so traffic could run in and out and around the city.

CITY HALL

POLICE DEP'T

GRAMMAR SCHOOL

LIBRARY

HIGH SCHOOL

CHURCH

PIGGERY

FIRE TOWER

ICE HOUSE

FIRE DEP'T

HOSPITAL

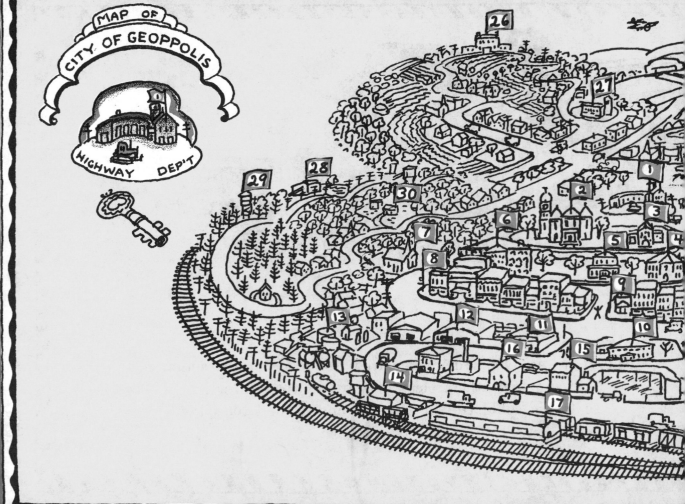

MAP OF
CITY OF GEOPPOLIS
HIGHWAY DEP'T

DAIRY FARM

WATER DEP'T

CHICKEN FARM

FACTORY

TELEPHONE CO.

ELECTRIC CO.

Katy also had a snow plow
to plow snow with.

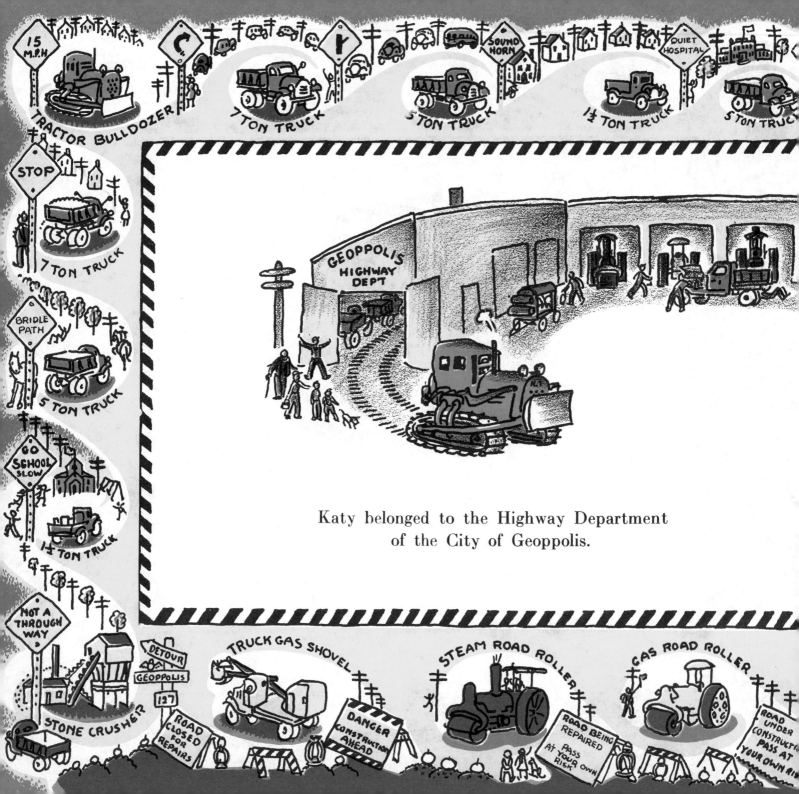

Katy belonged to the Highway Department
of the City of Geoppolis.

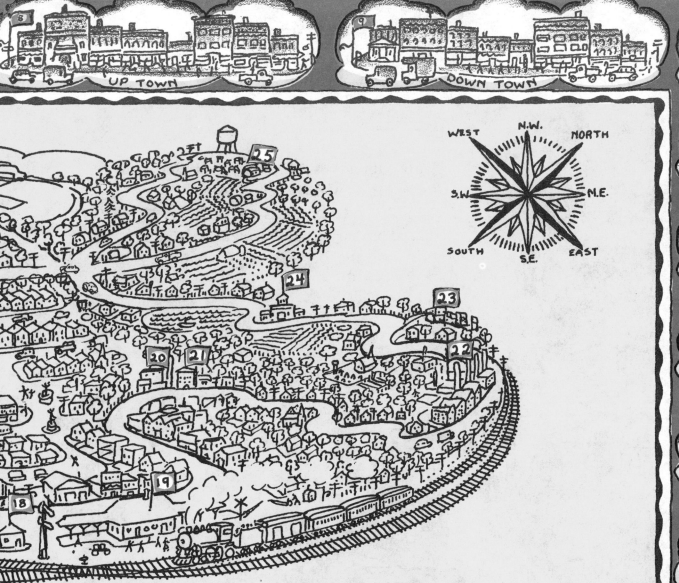

UP TOWN

DOWN TOWN

POST OFFICE

GARAGE

AUTO BUS

OIL

COAL

LUMBER

GEOPPOLIS RAILROAD STATION

RAILWAY EXPRESS

FREIGHT YARD

GRAIN

All summer Katy worked on the roads
with her bulldozer.
Katy liked to work.
The harder and tougher the job
the better she liked it.

Once when the steamroller fell in the pond
Katy pulled it out.
The Highway Department was very proud of her.
They used to say, "Nothing can stop her."

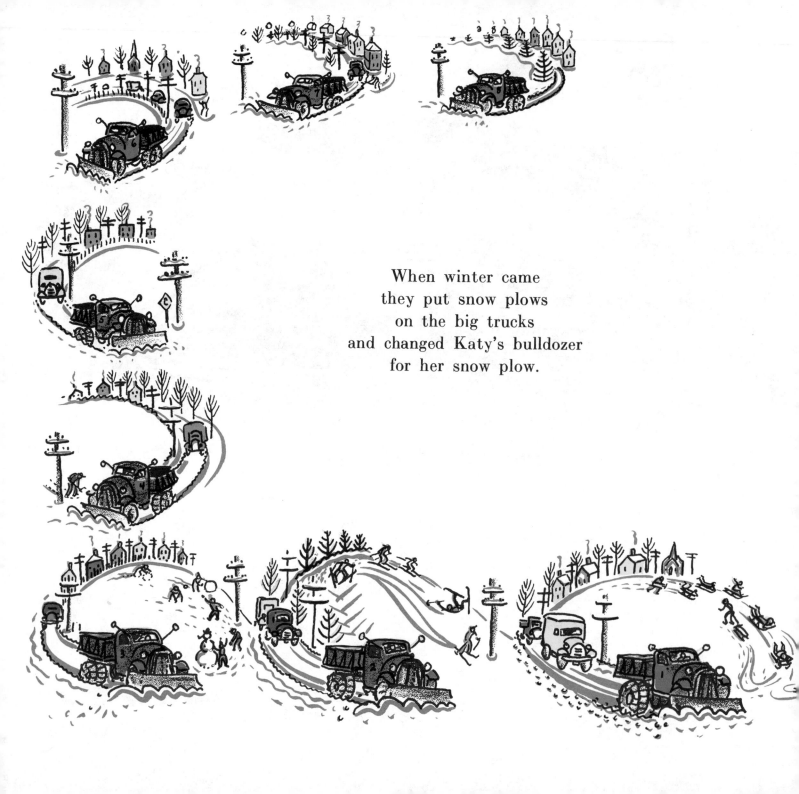

When winter came
they put snow plows
on the big trucks
and changed Katy's bulldozer
for her snow plow.

But Katy was so big and strong
she had to stay at home,
because there was not enough snow for her to plow.

Then early one morning it started to drizzle.
The drizzle turned into rain.
The rain turned into snow.
By noon it was four inches deep.
The Highway Department sent out the truck plows.

By afternoon the snow was ten inches deep
and still coming down.
"Looks like a Big Snow,"
they said at the Highway Department,
and sent Katy out.

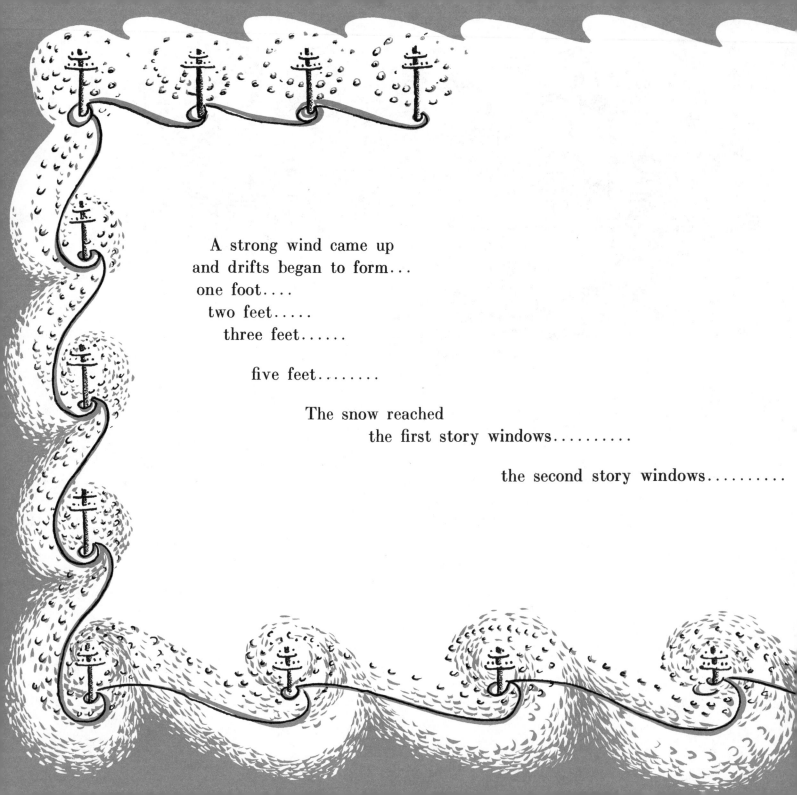

A strong wind came up
and drifts began to form...
one foot....
  two feet.....
    three feet......

      five feet........

        The snow reached
           the first story windows.........

              the second story windows.........

and then it stopped.
One by one the truck snow plows broke down....
The roads were blocked......
No traffic could move......
The schools, the stores, the factories were closed....
The railroad station and airport were snowed in....
The mail couldn't go through....
The Police couldn't protect the city....
The telephone and power lines were down...
There was a break in the water main...
The doctor couldn't get his patient to the hospital...
The Fire Department was helpless.....
Everyone and everything was stopped....
but...........

KATY

The City of Geoppolis was covered
with a thick blanket of snow.

Slowly and steadily
Katy started to plow out the city.

"Help!" called the Chief of Police.
"Help us to get out to protect the city."
"Sure," said Katy.   "Follow me."

So Katy plowed out the center of the city.

"Help," called out the Postmaster.
"Help us get the mail through."
"Sure," said Katy. "Follow me."

So Katy plowed down to the Railway Station.

"Help! Help!" called out the Telephone Company
and the Electric Company.
"The poles are down somewhere in East Geoppolis."
"Follow me," said Katy.

So Katy plowed out the roads to East Geoppolis.

"Help!"
called out the Superintendent of the Water Department.
"There's a break in the water main
somewhere in North Geoppolis."
"Follow me," said Katy

and she plowed out the roads to North Geoppolis.

"Help! Emergency!" called out the doctor.
"Help me get this patient to the hospital
way out in West Geoppolis."
"Sure," said Katy. "Follow me."

So Katy plowed out the roads to the hospital.

"Help! Help! Help!" called out the Fire Chief.
"There's a three alarm fire way out in South Geoppolis."
"Follow me," said Katy.

So Katy plowed out the roads to the fire in South Geoppolis.

On the way back a plane signalled for help.
The airport was snowed in.
Katy was beginning to get a little tired
but she wouldn't stop....
not Katy.

She hurried over to the airport
and plowed out the runways
so the airplane could land safely.

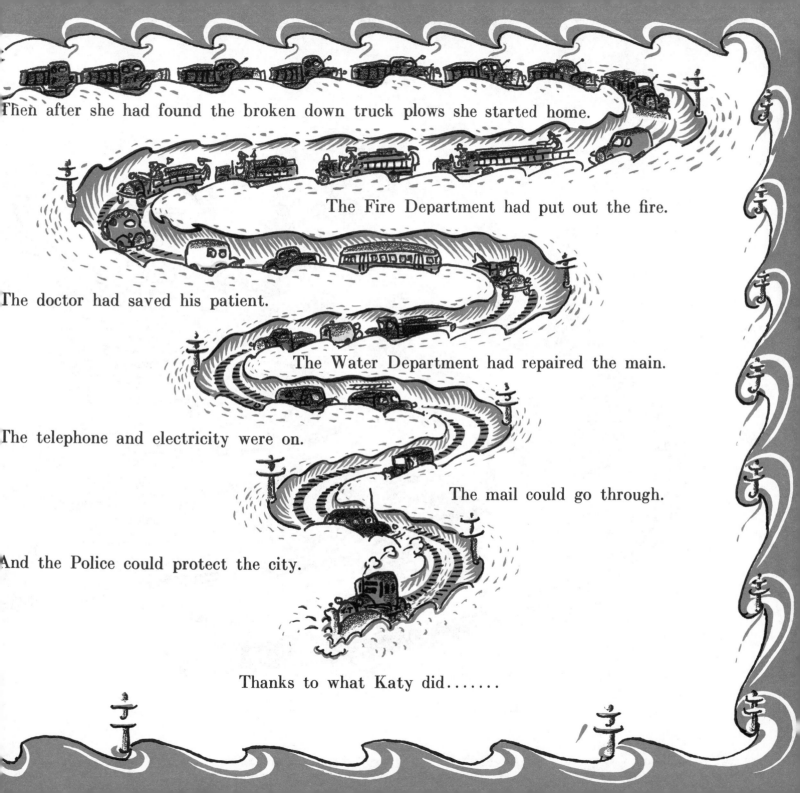

Then after she had found the broken down truck plows she started home.

The Fire Department had put out the fire.

The doctor had saved his patient.

The Water Department had repaired the main.

The telephone and electricity were on.

The mail could go through.

And the Police could protect the city.

Thanks to what Katy did.......

Katy finished up the side streets
so traffic could move in and out and around the city.
Then she went home to rest.
Then.....and only then did Katy stop.